A Tale of Christopher Corn
by Laurence M. Seitz

illustrated by Carina Reytblat

For Diane Seitz, the co-author of this book series. She was a loving wife, mother, and grandmother who dedicated her life as an advocate for children's health and safety.

"1st edition, 2nd book - eBook series
©Copyright 2022. All rights reserved."

Copyright © 2024 Laurence M. Seitz.

All Rights Reserved. No part of this book may be used or reproduced by any means, graphic, electronic, or mechanical, including photocopying, recording, taping, or by any information storage retrieval system without the written permission of the author, except in the case of brief quotations embodied in critical articles and reviews.

SunPower Kidz®books may be ordered through booksellers or by contacting **www.sun-powerkidz.com.**

ISBN: 978-2-7193-1249-0 (sc)
ISBN: 978-2-9937-0819-0 (hc)
ISBN: 978-2-09114991-0 (e)

Library of Congress Control Number: 2023921985

SunPower Kidz®

A Dream Come True

Thirty-three years ago, I had a dream that focused on the world of a child. I wondered how I could offer children from all over the world, using 3-D graphics and animation, an opportunity in a creative way to understand the importance of natural food for a healthy body.

This passion led to the creative world of the SunPower Kidz®. The brand's mission was manifested in the first thirty-six characters. Representing fruits, dairy products, vegetables, proteins, and grains each one came to life. A child's imagination took over as each portrayed this unique character and dressed them selves in an activity that a child desired to become. Children learned the depth of what each SunPower Kidz® offered. Children adopted their favorite character. By dressing in their favored activity they experienced a healthy approach to food, nutrition, and family values represented in each tale.

As tales were told, beautiful original illustrations brought characters to life. Audiobooks with original songs were created. Each different tale presented important lessons of life. Therefore, each child using the power of imagination became the healthy essence of its favorite character. Thus, this created a unique, positive, and healthy direction for their future.

Laurence M. Seitz
CEO/Founder

CONTENTS

The Day's Plan chapter 1

Pelican Beach chapter 2

A Painful Trip Home chapter 3

Home chapter 4

Christopher Corn raced down the staircase from his bedroom.

He approached his mother and father, who were reading in the living room.

"Mom, Dad, I'm going to the beach with my friends. Okay?" asked Christopher. "I'll be home before the sun goes down."

"Whom are you going with?" asked his father.

"Which beach are you going to?" asked his mother. "Who's taking you there?"

"I'm going with my friends to Pelican Beach. We can walk there," answered Christopher. "It's not that far."

"This is the first weekend since school let out for the summer, the beach will certainly be crowded," acknowledged Mother Corn.

"Yep," answered Christopher, hopping from one foot to the other with excitement. "That's why my friends and I are going as early as possible, so we can get a good spot before the older kids show up."

"Okay. Just be careful, and please remember to keep your husk on," reminded Mother Corn. "That sun can be dangerous, and you blister so easily."

"Yes, I know, Mom," said Christopher with a touch of sarcasm. "You've told me that a hundred times."

"Son, listen to your mother," said Father Corn sternly. "Yes, Dad," replied Christopher, eager to get going. "I'll remember."

"Okay honey. Have fun," said Mother Corn, giving him a warm hug. "Yup. Have to go. Bye!" Christopher said, dashing out of the house.

"Christopher certainly is a kernel off the old cob." Mother Corn smiled and slightly shook her head.

"We told him what to do for his safety," said Father Corn.
"That's what loving parents do."

Father corn returned to reading his book, "The History of Ethanol", as Mother corn stood up.

"I've got to finish the laundry, dear," she said.

Father corn mumbled something that sounded like, "Yes, dear," and kept reading.

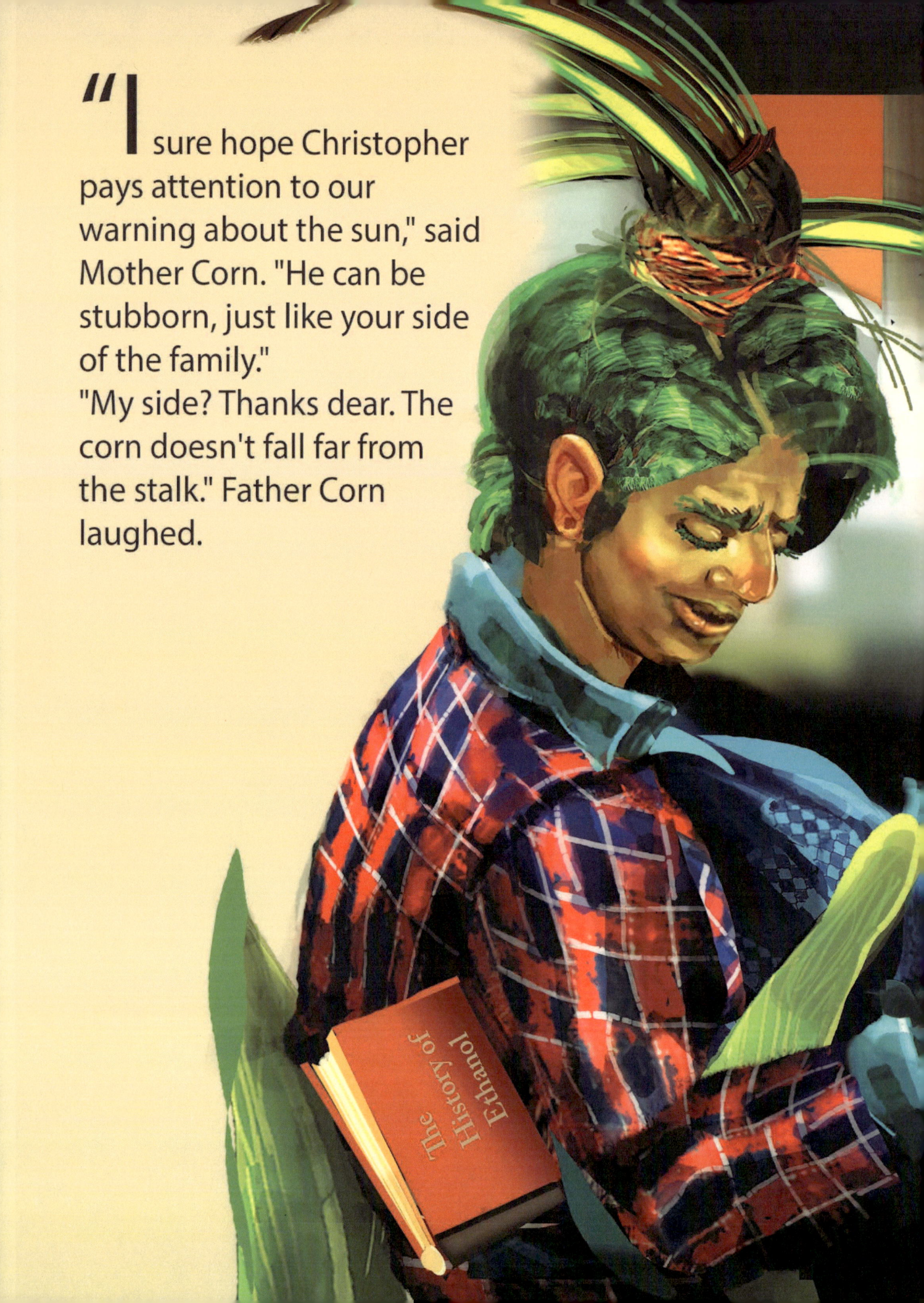

"I sure hope Christopher pays attention to our warning about the sun," said Mother Corn. "He can be stubborn, just like your side of the family."
"My side? Thanks dear. The corn doesn't fall far from the stalk." Father Corn laughed.

Mother Corn went into the laundry room. She looked back and said, "Why don't you think what you would like for lunch?"

"Thank you, honey," said Father Corn. "That's a thoughtful suggestion."

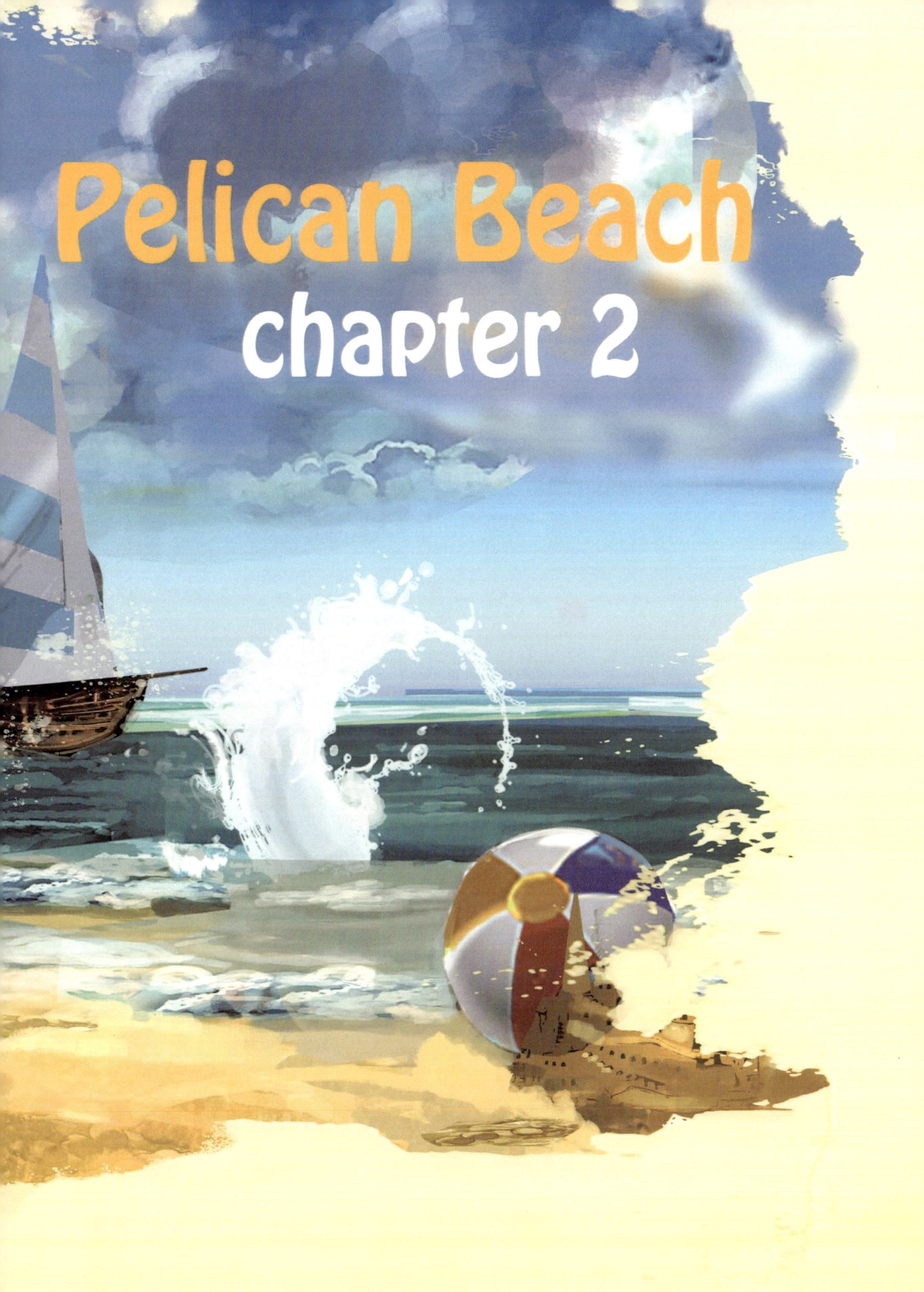

Meanwhile, at the beach, there was a cool breeze blowing in from the ocean, keeping everyone from feeling the sun's powerful rays on their kernels.
Since it wasn't so hot, one by one, all of Christopher's friends removed their husks.

"Hey Christopher," asked Cassandra Corn. "How come you're not taking your husk off?"

"Yeah," budded in Charlie Corn, one of the older corns, teasing Christopher with a smirk on his face.

"What are you afraid of Christopher?"

Christopher looked at the sand, giving the question some thought.

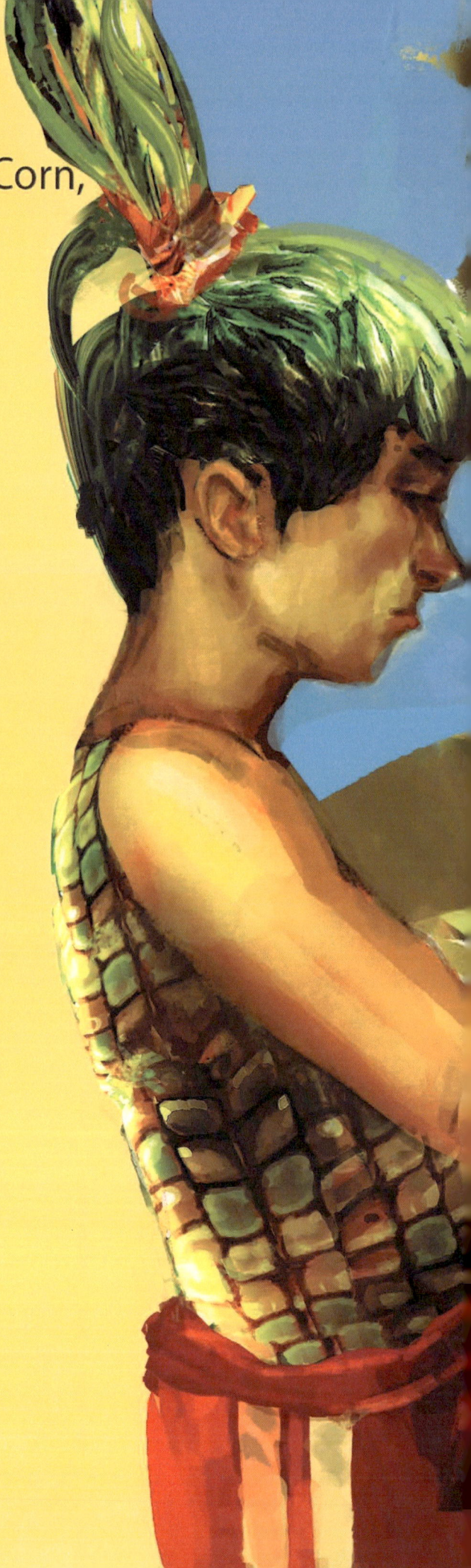

"He's afraid his Mommy and Daddy will yell at him because he didn't listen to them, right Christopher?" taunted Charlie, remembering how his parents had yelled at him last summer when he took off his husk and all of his kernels popped.

"No. That's not true," said Christopher, uncomfortable with everyone's eyes on him. "I'll take it off right now," he said boldly, exposing his kernels to the hot sun. "Now you're cool like us," said Charlie Corn.

"Last one into the water is an old cob," shouted Chico Corn, racing toward the ocean. A dozen ears of corn followed diving into the surf. It was quite a sight!

For the rest of the day, Christopher and his friends frolicked in the ocean. Splashing, bobbing, and floating lazily in the cool ocean water.

Then it happened. "Pop. Pop, pop, pop!" Christopher's kernels started blowing up as blisters formed all over his cob. He put on his husk, trying to block out the powerful rays of the sun, but it was too late!"

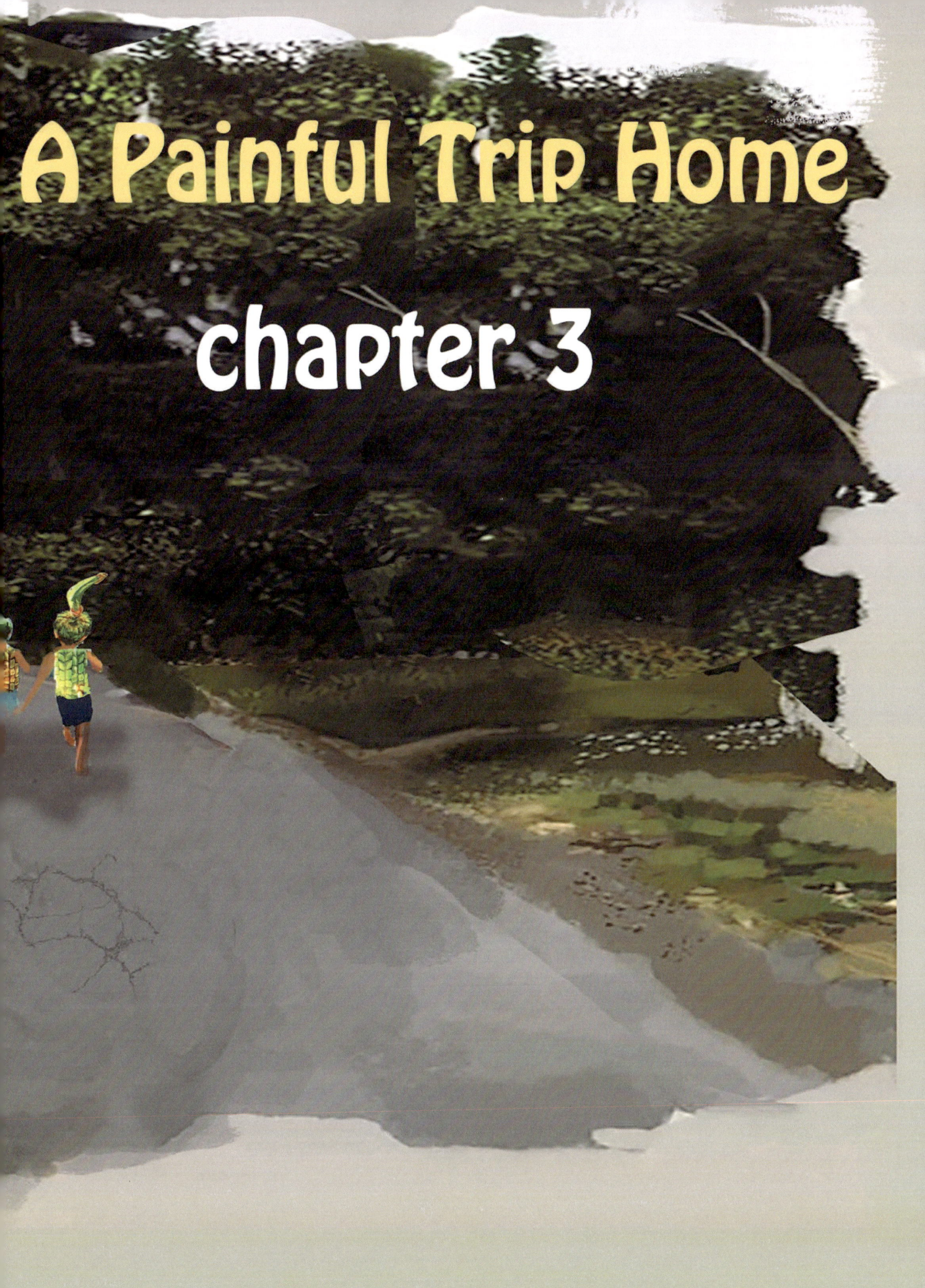

On the long walk home, his friend, Catyln, walked up to him. "We shouldn't have listened to those older corns," she whispered. "I hurt all over." Christopher acknowledged her with a nod and a long sigh.

"It was so painful when I put my husk back on," she said.

"I know," said Christopher weakly grimacing in pain. His cob had popped kernels all over, and his husk rubbed painfully against them with every step he took.

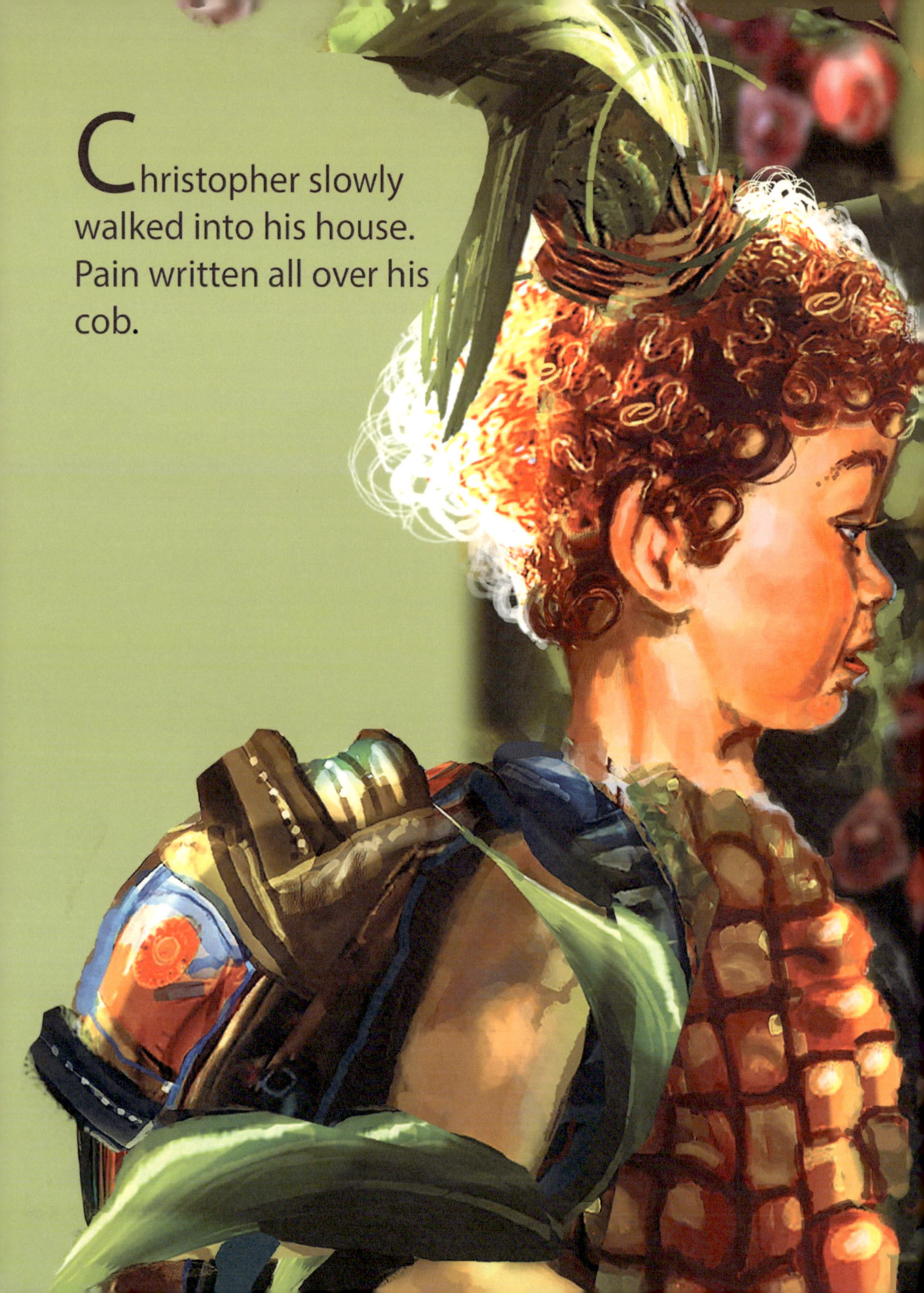

Christopher slowly walked into his house. Pain written all over his cob.

One look from his parents and he began to cry. Christopher knew he paid the price for ignoring his parents warnings.
He stood in front of them with a lowered head and said, "I'm not sure what hurts more. My blisters or not listening to you.

"Your mother warned you," Father Corn said. "Son, why didn't you listen to us?"
"I did, Dad. I kept my husk on, b-b-but, there were these older kids there too, and they kept on making fun of me," explained Christopher. "I felt so odd with everyone looking at me."

"Christopher, there is a lesson to be learned today," said Father Corn. "Their words are empty."

"What does that mean?" asked Christopher. "How could words be empty?"

"Words are empty when they make you feel uncomfortable," advised his father. "The words of your mother and I would never do that. You experienced being bullied."

"Yes father. Now that you say it," nodded Christopher. "I definitely had that uncomfortable feeling as they made fun of me."

"Always be true to yourself. Listen to your heart," added Mother Corn. "Our words are filled with love and experience."

Mother Corn stood up, walked over to her whimpering son and wiped his tears.
Carefully, she helped Christopher lower his husk. "It's OK, Christopher. You'll be fine," said his mother.

"You're right Mom and Dad," said Christopher. "If I had listened to your warnings and ignored their empty words, I wouldn't be suffering now."
"Mom...Dad...more than anything I want to hug you," said Christopher.
Then the strangest thing happened. His pain began to ease as his popped kernels began to recede.

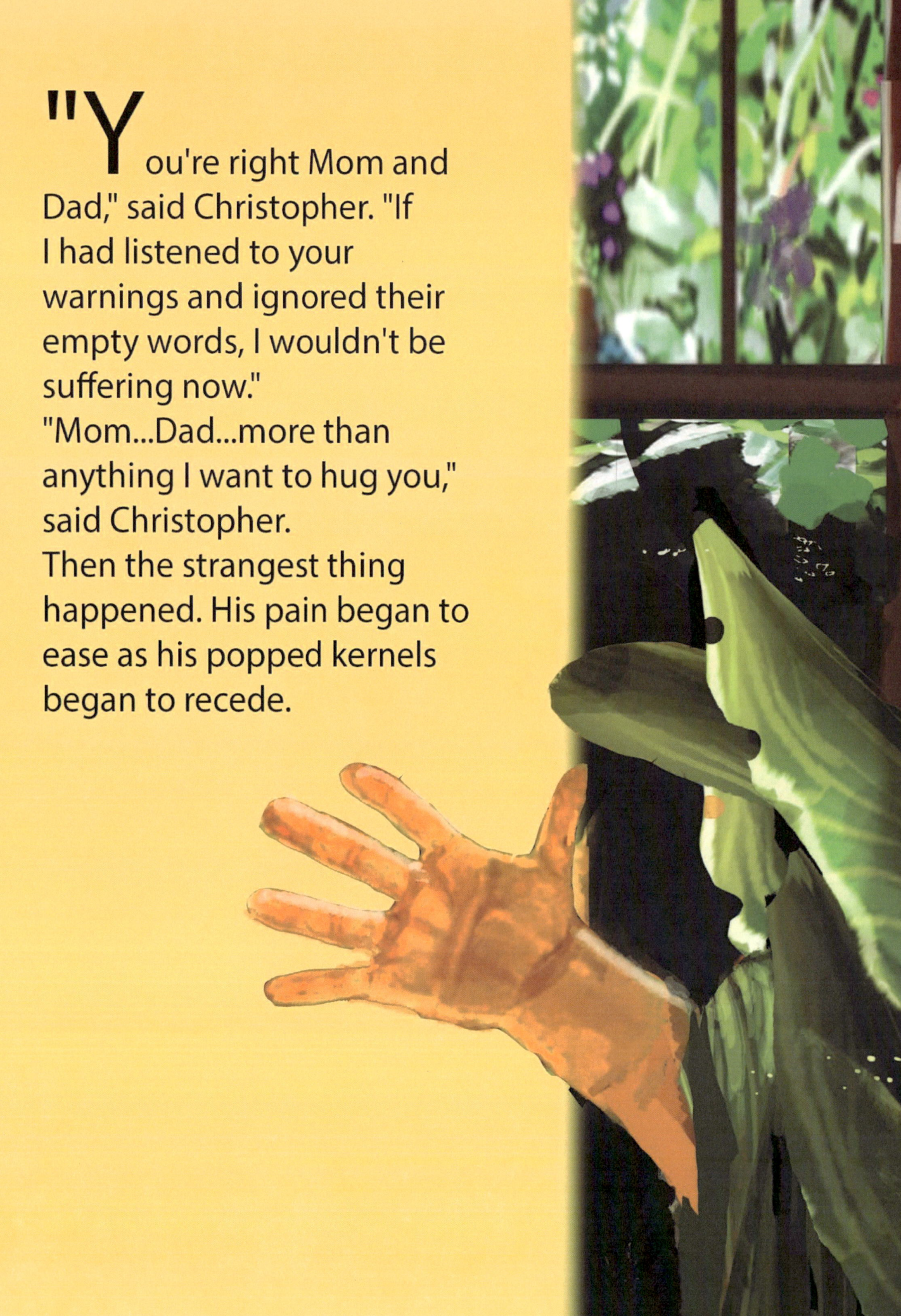

His parents came over with loving smiles and wrapped him into a love filled, tight hug.
As Christopher stood there, surround by his parent's warmth and love, he made sure he would always remember the valuable lessons he had learned that day. He would never forget the power of words, listening to one's parents, recognizing when one is being bullied, and the meaning of feeling uncomfortable when someone offers empty words.

About the Author

Laurence Seitz is a Physical Therapist. His dedication to his patients has spanned many decades. This devotion to all ages became the genesis of the SunPower Kidz®. Now he has written a book series established as an international treasure for children.

When he is not writing or creating songs, he is engaged with computer, 3-D modeling and animation, gardening and raising fruits and vegetables. He enjoys music of all genres and is an avid New York sports fan.

Tales of the first SunPower Kidz® book series.

Diane's Legacy for Children

OLIVER ORANGE™-teaches us about real friendship as you witness an incredible act of selfless kindness and bravery. Friendship has nothing to do with size, words, or skill. Oliver showed he is a true friend regardless of how unkind others were to him.

CHRISTOPHER CORN™-understood that words are empty when they make you feel uncomfortable and offer pain. Empty words only encourage being bullied. One should always be true to oneself. Listen to your heart. For then words are filled with love, truth, and kindness, and the role one's parents play.

PENELOPE PEAR™-learned that in her world everyone is a pear. No matter where one came from or looked like, we must always respect each other 'and our differences. Being brown, red, green, or whatever color a pear is doesn't matter, because we are all pears. We must always look past our external appearance and see what's inside.

BETTY BROCCOLI™-experienced the hurtful words of being bullied in school. Offered loving words from her mother and friends taught her to love herself and be proud of unique differences. She learned self respect and how to ignore painful and foolish words.

The cast of "A Tale of Christopher Corn"™

Christopher Corn

Mother Corn

Casey Corn

Chico Corn

Father Corn

Cassandra Corn

Catyln Corn

Charlie Corn

Recipes

1. Corn and Cheese Quesadillas: Spread shredded cheese and corn kernels on a tortilla, fold it in half, and cook it on a pan until the cheese melts and the tortilla is crispy.

2. Corn Salad: Mix cooked corn kernels with diced tomatoes, cucumbers, and bell peppers. Drizzle with a light dressing made of olive oil, lime juice, salt, and pepper.

3. Corn Fritters: In a bowl, combine corn kernels, flour, egg, milk, salt, and pepper. Heat oil in a pan, drop spoonfuls of the batter into the pan, and cook until golden brown on both sides.

4. Corn and Chicken Wrap: Spread cream cheese on a tortilla, add cooked shredded chicken, corn kernels, and lettuce. Roll it up tightly and cut into bite-sized pieces.

5. Corn on the Cob with Herbed Butter: Boil corn on the cob until tender. In a small bowl, mix softened butter with minced herbs like parsley, chives, or cilantro. Spread the herbed butter on the corn for extra flavor.

These recipes are simple, delicious, and a great way to incorporate corn into your child's meals. Enjoy cooking with them!

The Evolution of SunPower Kidz ®

SunPower Kidz®

Abigall Apple™    Arthur Artichoke™    Cristopher Corn  ™   Penelope Pear™

Rachel Raspberry™    Percy Pumpkin™    Charlie Cantaloupe™    Eddie Eggplant™

Wally Watermelon™    Stacie Strawberry™    Priscilla Peach™    Daniel Date™

Chelsea Cherry™    Gracie Grape™    Larry Lime™

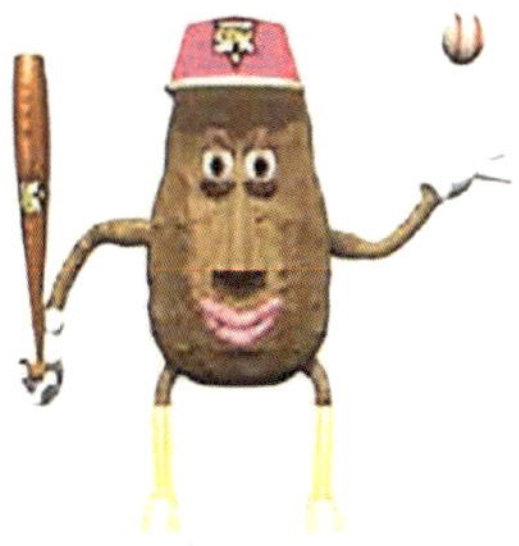

Peter Potato™

A poem about Christopher Corn

In the realm of SunPower Kidz®, radiant and bold,
Lives Christopher Corn™, with a story to be told.
A SunPower Kidz, full of zest and grace,
With a love for wholesome food, he takes his place.

Christopher Corn, a maestro of the fields,
Where golden grains sway and nature yields.
With every stalk that dances in the breeze,
He tends to the crops, nurturing with ease.

In the heart of harvest, his spirit shines bright,
Guiding children toward a healthy, joyful flight.
With songs of nutrition, he fills the air,
Teaching kids to embrace meals that truly care.

A symphony of flavors, he brings to the plate,
Turns grains into feasts, early and late.
From hearty bread to dishes divine,
Christopher Corn's creations always shine.

In the garden's embrace, he finds his home,
Where SunPower Kidz values brightly roam.
With every harvest, every grain that's born,
Christopher Corn, a SunPower Kidz sworn.

So here's to Christopher Corn, a symbol so true,
Teaching kids to nourish, to grow and renew.
In the world of SunPower Kidz, where health is in bloom,
He leads the way, banishing nutritional gloom.

www.ingramcontent.com/pod-product-compliance
Lightning Source LLC
LaVergne TN
LVRC092314110526
838202LV00108B/2624